Where Animals Live

The World of Hummingbirds

Words by Robert Brown

Adapted from Susan Quimby Foster's
The Hummingbird in the Flowers

Photographs by
Wendy Shattil and Bob Rozinski/
Oxford Scientific Films

Gareth Stevens Publishing
Milwaukee

Contents

Note: The use of a capital letter for a hummingbird's name means that it is a *species*, or type, of hummingbird (for example, Rufous Hummingbird). The use of a lowercase, or small, letter means that it is a member of a larger *group* of hummingbirds.

The Whirring of Wings

The sound of hummingbird wings can be heard wherever wildflowers bloom in North and South America. There are about 320 *species* in the large hummingbird family. These species range from the southern tip of South America to southern Alaska.

Hummingbirds are among the smallest birds in the world. They range from the size of a large bee (the Cuban Bee Hummingbird) all the way to the length of a starling (the Giant Humming-bird of South America).

Although hummingbirds appear frail, they are tough little birds. Some live at 15,000 ft (4,600 m) high up in the Andes in Peru.

The Hummingbird's Body

Hummingbirds have streamlined bodies and metallic-colored feathers. Some males have a beautiful patch of feathers on the throat, called a *gorget*. Others have brightly colored feathers and streaming tail feathers.

All hummingbirds have tiny feet which they can use to perch and comb their feathers. Because they cannot hop or walk very well, humming-birds seldom land on the ground. When moving farther than just a few inches, these little birds take to the air.

Hummingbirds feed on nectar. They use their beaks to reach nectar deep inside all sorts of different flowers.

Hummingbirds have very long tongues. Their tongues can stretch out twice as long as their beaks. They can lick up nectar at the lickety-split rate of 13 licks per second.

The humming sound that hummingbirds make comes from the vibration of their wings. As they beat their wings, air passes through notches in their feathers. A hummingbird can also make noises by using the voice box in its throat.

Hummingbirds have very strong chest muscles that give the bird the power to fly. Its wings beat so fast that we see only a blur. By using slow-motion photography, we can see their wing movement.

A hummingbird needs more food energy than any other bird. Easily digested flower nectars are a ready source of food for this always hungry bird.

Hummingbirds must maintain their body temperature between 104° and 110°F (40°-43°C). In hot weather, they cool themselves by panting like dogs. On cold nights, they can die because they have no *insulating* feathers to keep them warm. Because they are so small, bad weather may prevent them from flying and finding food.

Jewels in the Sky

Male hummingbirds are among the most brilliantly colored animals in the world. Their feathers glisten and shimmer as if the birds are wearing precious jewels. Since females spend much of their time nesting, their feathers are less colorful.

When a hummingbird *preens*, it uses its beak and claws to smooth its feathers. In this way, it tames its unruly feathers into silky smoothness.

As you watch a hummingbird, you will see the feathers change colors as the bird moves. The color depends on how the sunlight shines and reflects on the surface of the feathers.

In direct sunlight, the gorget of a male Broad-tailed Hummingbird seems to sparkle with a red color (left). But the gorget changes to black when it is in shadow (right).

The sparkling effect on this bird's gorget is caused by light reflecting from tiny "mirrors" in each feather.

The Living Helicopters

Unlike other birds, hummingbirds have stiff wings. But their shoulder joints are quite flexible. They allow each wing to turn over completely, like an oar, on each wing beat.

Hummingbirds change direction by pivoting their wings and tilting their bodies at different angles. Their flight is further controlled by the tilting and fanning out of the tail feathers.

Hovering   Forward   Upward   Backward

A small hummingbird like this Rufous Humming-bird is held in midair by beating its wings between 38 and 78 times per second.

Hummingbirds are the acrobats of the skies. No other bird can accelerate instantly from a hover to full speed.

A Broadtailed Hummingbird's wings move in figure eights as the bird hovers at a flower (lower left). Wings tracing tiny ovals in the air guide this Hermit Hummingbird forward to a flower (lower right).

Hummingbird Flowers

Hummingbirds feed only from certain kinds of flowers. These special hummingbird flowers are often red with beautiful blossoms that attract the birds. A long, tubular petal keeps the nectar beyond the reach of butterfly tongues and burrowing bees.

Hummingbirds and their flowers are made for each other. The bird's slender head, long beak, and extendable tongue can reach deep inside the blossom.

Hummingbirds feed greedily when penstemons  (left) and other wildflowers are in bloom. The red and orange tubular flowers of the Ocotillo (right) are also attractive to hummingbirds.

Nectar is about one-quarter sugar. It is a valuable food that provides energy for hummingbirds. Hummingbirds actually help these plants reproduce by carrying *pollen* from one flower to another of the same species. This process is called *pollination*.

Hovering safely above dangerous spines, a bird sips nectar, pollen, and insects from the flower of a Claret Cup Cactus.

The Hummingbird's Appetite

Hummingbirds spend most of their time searching for food. The Anna's Hummingbird (above) feeds from over 1,000 flowers each day.

Hummingbirds are *omnivores* and need to eat animal proteins as well as nectar. They catch insects by swiping them from the air or plucking them from spiderwebs and flowers. But this hummingbird's favorite food (below) is nectar, which provides it with water, sugar, vitamins, and minerals.

Hummingbirds quickly learn which flowers produce the sweetest nectar. Nectar deep at the base of the passionflower is reached only by the Long-tailed Hermit's tapered beak.

In addition to nectar, hummingbirds need oxygen to survive. They use up oxygen more quickly than any other animal. A perching bird breathes about 250 times per minute (humans breathe about 17 times a minute when at rest). The bird's heart pumps sugar and oxygen through its body at about 500 beats a minute when at rest (human hearts beat about 60 times a minute when at rest).

The Long-distance Travelers

Most hummingbirds stay all year in the rain forests of Central and South America. But there are 21 species of hummingbirds that migrate to North America each spring.

In North America, hummingbirds have less competition for breeding sites and food. Each fall, these migrating birds avoid harsh winters by returning south to the tropics.

This Rufous Hummingbird is no larger than your thumb. It migrates from Central America to Alaska, traveling about 2,500 miles (4,000 km) each way during its journey each year.

This migrating hummingbird remembers good places to eat and returns to those places year after year.

Claiming a Territory

In spring and early summer, hummingbirds perch only briefly to rest (upper left). During this time, they fight for good sources of nectar. When hummingbirds fight, they dart and somersault through the air until one is declared the winner.

In this quarrelsome, unfriendly manner, a male hummingbird becomes the owner of a feeding territory. Following spring migration, the male Broadtailed Hummingbird establishes and fiercely defends its food sources.

This female Broadtailed Hummingbird enters the male's territory to feed, then quickly whirs away. Males sometimes chase fleeing females into shrubs, where they mate.

To protect his territory, a male Broadtailed Hummingbird performs a flying show called an *aerial display*. During this display, a Broadtail screeches and plummets headfirst toward the ground. The dive is broken off just a few feet from certain death.

If you are wearing something red, a diving Broadtail may zoom like a missile past your ears or stop to hover curiously right before your nose. It will mistake you for a large flower!

Nesting and Laying Eggs

This Broadtailed Hummingbird's nest is a cozy collection of cobwebs, lichens, insect cocoons, and pine needles. The nest is molded by the mother bird's beak and body.

A female hummingbird builds her nest on tree branches, leaves, or vines with sticky spider-webs. She weaves fibers together using her beak and claws. This tiny hummingbird nest blends in so well with branches and leaves that it is quite difficult to see.

When it is done, the nest opening is barely two inches (5 cm) wide. You can see how small a hummingbird egg is compared to a chicken egg. In fact, the hummingbird's nest is not even as big as a chicken egg! An average hummingbird egg is less than 1/2 inch (1.2 cm) long and weighs only about 1/50th of an ounce (1/2 gram).

Female hummingbirds lay two eggs, usually two days apart. If baby birds are to hatch, the eggs must be *incubated*. The female warms them by nestling her breast against them for about 80 percent of each day. This incubation period lasts for 15 to 22 days. Each developing baby is nourished by the rich yolk inside the egg.

Baby Birds in the Nest

After 15 to 22 days, the baby chicks hatch. Helped by strong neck muscles and a chisel-like tooth on the beak, each baby bird taps the inside of the shell until it cracks open. These two Broadtailed Hummingbirds (upper left) huddle together for warmth while their mother searches for food.

The chicks are naked, blind, and helpless when they first hatch. The mother snuggles and warms her babies by *brooding* them.

The begging chicks (opposite, right) gape open their mouths the instant their mother returns. She feeds them by *regurgitating* a mixture of nectar and insects she has stored in her *crop*.

After about 10 days, the chicks are covered with feathers. They then begin to stretch their wings and exercise their long tongues. When they are 21 days old, they suddenly take flight below. When they are about six weeks old, they are ready to find food on their own.

Friends and Neighbors

Wasps, butterflies, ants, and bees share the
hummingbird's thirst for nectar. Some bees
chew through petals to reach the honey pot at
the base of the flower.

Hummingbirds have a curious relationship
with a group of tiny animals called mites. These
creatures live and breed inside hummingbird
flowers. As many as twelve mites may jump
aboard a feeding hummingbird and hitch a ride
to the next flower. There, they scoot down the
bird's beak to the petals. The hummingbird
serves as an airplane for the mites, carrying
them to new supplies of food.

↑

The sticky silk of a spider's web is an ideal building material for a hummingbird nest.

Many people attract hummingbirds to their houses by planting hummingbird flowers or setting out hummingbird feeders. This hungry gray squirrel is stealing sugar water from a hummingbird feeder. ↓

Predators and Other Dangers

Most hummingbirds can escape any animal that tries to catch them. Even so, these nimble birds must always be on the alert for *predators* such as falcons, dragonflies, frogs, and fish. This American Kestrel (above) occasionally catches an unwary hummingbird.

The acrobatic hummingbird is no match for this Peregrine Falcon, which reaches 200 mph (320 kph) during a dive.

Hummingbirds may also become the victims of other disasters. Some crash into windows, while others are poisoned by chemicals.

Severe weather and cold nights can kill hummingbirds. But they can survive these hard times by passing into *torpor*. In torpor, a bird requires only 1/50th of its normal demand for energy.

Hummingbirds and People ⬆

Hummingbirds have been admired by native peoples of Central and South America for thousands of years. This hummingbird mask (above left) once belonged to an Apache Indian. A modern American Indian artist, Robert Sebastian, has painted his version of a hummingbird on a silk screen (above right).

The Hopi Indians of Arizona carved dolls called kachinas in the likeness of hummingbirds to use in their ceremonies. ➡

When Europeans came to the Americas, they were impressed by the unusual beauty of hummingbirds. They wanted specimens to study, admire, and display. Sadly, some people saw the chance to make money out of these little birds. Hummingbirds were killed for their feathers, which were used to decorate fans, necklaces, and hats.

Fortunately, the United States and some Latin American countries now protect hummingbirds and other endangered wildlife.

Life among the Flowers

Hummingbirds share their *habitat* with many other plants and animals. While feeding on insects and the nectar of plants, hummingbirds in turn may be eaten by predators such as the American Kestrel or Leopard Frog. This diagram outlines the hummingbird's place in the food chain.

Food Chain

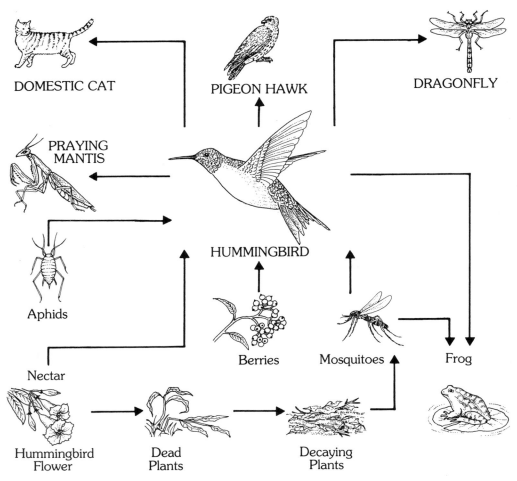

DOMESTIC CAT

PIGEON HAWK

DRAGONFLY

PRAYING MANTIS

HUMMINGBIRD

Aphids

Berries

Mosquitoes

Frog

Nectar

Hummingbird Flower

Dead Plants

Decaying Plants

Hummingbirds can live for up to ten years in the wild. During this time, they provide plants with an important service. For example, in the southwestern US, 129 species of flowering plants depend on hummingbirds for pollination.

We are amused by hummingbirds' curiosity and thrilled by their dazzling colors and dramatic flying displays. Hummingbirds enrich the lives of all who value the wonders of the natural world.

Index and New Words About Hummingbirds

These new words about hummingbirds appear in the text on the pages shown after each definition. Each new word first appears in the text in *italics*, just as it appears here.

aerial display . a series of flight patterns performed by male hummingbirds. **19**

brooding ...... protective behavior of birds by which the young are warmed and sheltered beneath the wings and body of a parent. **22**

crop .... in birds, a pouchlike sac in which food may be stored or partially digested. **23**

gorget .... a region of colorful feathers between the beak and the belly on a male hummingbird. **4, 9**

habitat .... an area that provides an animal with food, shelter, water, and adequate space. **30**

incubated ..... (of eggs) kept warm so they will hatch. **21**

insulating ..... preventing the transfer of heat into or out of an object or a living thing. **7**

nectar .... a sugary syrup secreted by some kinds of flowers. **5, 7, 12, 13-15, 18, 23, 24**

omnivore ...... an animal that eats both plants and other animals. **14**

pollen .... a fine powder produced on a flower's anthers. **13**

pollination ... the process by which pollen is transferred from the anther of one flower to the pistil of another. Pollination results in fertilization and the formation of a seed. **13, 31**

predator .... an animal that survives primarily by eating other animals. **26**

preen .... to rearrange and smooth the feathers. **8**

regurgitate ... for a mother bird, to bring up undigested food from her stomach to feed chicks. **23**

species .... a group of living things with similar features that are able to breed and produce off-spring among their own kind. **2, 3, 16, 31**

torpor .... a state of lowered body function that allows hummingbirds to survive cold nights and severe weather conditions. **27**

Reading level analysis: SPACHE 3.5, FRY 5, FLESCH 89 (easy), FOG 4, SMOG 3

Library of Congress Cataloging-in-Publication Data

Brown, Robert, 1961-
 The world of hummingbirds / words by Robert Brown; photographs by Oxford Scientific Films.
  p. cm. – (Where animals live)
 "Adapted from Susan Q. Foster's The hummingbird among the flowers."
 Summary: Text and photographs illustrate the lives of hummingbirds in their natural settings, describing how they feed, defend themselves, and breed.
 ISBN 0-8368-0140-7
 1. Hummingbirds--Juvenile literature. [1. Hummingbirds.] I. Foster, Susan Q. Hummingbird among the flowers. II. Oxford Scientific Films. III. Title. IV. Series.
QL696.A558H37   1989
598.8'99--dc20   89-31913

North American edition first published in 1990 by Gareth Stevens Children's Books, RiverCenter Building, Suite 201, 1555 North RiverCenter Drive, Milwaukee, WI 53212, USA
US edition, this format, copyright © 1989 by Belitha Press Ltd. Text copyright © 1990 by Gareth Stevens, Inc. All rights reserved. No part of this book may be reproduced in any form or by any means without permission in writing from Gareth Stevens, Inc.
First conceived, designed, and produced by Belitha Press Ltd., London, as **The Hummingbird among the Flowers**, with an original text copyright by Oxford Scientific Films. Format copyright by Belitha Press Ltd.
Series Editors: Mark J. Sachner and Carol Watson. Art Director: Treld Bicknell. Design: Naomi Games. Cover Design: Gary Moseley. Line Drawings: Lorna Turpin.

The author and publishers wish to thank the following for permission to reproduce copyright material: **Wendy Shattil and Bob Rozinski** for title page, pp. 3, 5, 7, 9 all, 10, 11 right, 12 both, 13, 14 below, 18 both, 19, 20 both, 21 both, 22 both, 23, 24 both, 25 both, 26, 27, 28 both, 29, 31, and front and back covers; **Oxford Scientific Films Ltd.** for p. 2 (S. R. Morris); pp. 4 and 6 (Tom Ulrich); p. 8 (Stephen Dalton); p. 14 above (Animals Animals — Alan G. Nelson); p. 15 (Michael Fogden); p. 17 (Bruce A. MacDonald); Partridge Films Ltd. for pp. 11 left (Carol Farnetti) and 16 (Richard Foster). Pages 28 both and 29 are courtesy of the Denver Museum of Natural History.

Printed in the United States of America
1 2 3 4 5 6 7 8 9 96 95 94 93 92 91 90
For a free color catalog describing Gareth Stevens' list of high-quality children's books, call 1-800-341-3569.

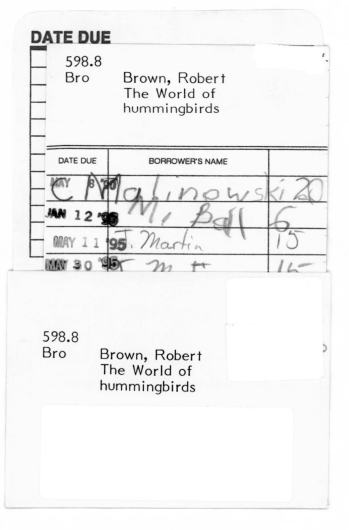

DATE DUE

598.8
Bro

Brown, Robert
The World of
hummingbirds

DATE DUE	BORROWER'S NAME	
MAY 8 '90	C Malinowski	20
JAN 12 '95	M, Ball	6
MAY 11 '95	J. Martin	15
MAY 30 '95	m t	16

598.8
Bro

Brown, Robert
The World of
hummingbirds